C S B
S C R I P T U R E
N O T E B O O K

2 Corinthians

Read. Reflect. Respond.

CSB CHRISTIAN STANDARD BIBLE® | HOLMAN® BIBLES

2 CORINTHIANS

Greeting

1 Paul, an apostle of Christ Jesus by God's will, and Timothy our brother:

To the church of God at Corinth, with all the saints who are throughout Achaia.

² Grace to you and peace from God our Father and the Lord Jesus Christ.

The God of Comfort

³ Blessed be the God and Father of our Lord Jesus Christ, the Father of mercies and the God of all comfort. ⁴ He comforts us in all our affliction, so that we may be able to comfort those who are in any kind of affliction, through the comfort we ourselves receive from God. ⁵ For just as the sufferings of Christ overflow to us, so also through Christ our comfort overflows. ⁶ If we are afflicted, it is for your comfort and salvation. If we are comforted, it is for your comfort, which produces in you patient endurance of the same sufferings that we suffer. ⁷ And our hope for you is firm, because we know that as you share in the sufferings, so you will also share in the comfort.

⁸ We don't want you to be unaware, brothers and sisters, of our affliction that took place in Asia. We were completely overwhelmed — beyond our strength — so that we even despaired of life itself. ⁹ Indeed, we felt that we had received the sentence of death, so that we would not trust in ourselves but in God who raises the dead. ¹⁰ He has delivered us from such a terrible death, and he will deliver us. We have put our hope in him that he will deliver us again ¹¹ while you join in helping us by your prayers. Then many will give thanks on our behalf for the gift that came to us through the prayers of many.

A Clear Conscience

¹² Indeed, this is our boast: The testimony of our conscience is

that we have conducted ourselves in the world, and especially toward you, with godly sincerity and purity, not by human wisdom but by God's grace. [13] For we are writing nothing to you other than what you can read and also understand. I hope you will understand completely — [14] just as you have partially understood us — that we are your reason for pride, just as you also are ours in the day of our Lord Jesus.

A Visit Postponed

[15] Because of this confidence, I planned to come to you first, so that you could have a second benefit, [16] and to visit you on my way to Macedonia, and then come to you again from Macedonia and be helped by you on my journey to Judea. [17] Now when I planned this, was I of two minds? Or what I plan, do I plan in a purely human way so that I say "Yes, yes" and "No, no" at the same time? [18] As God is faithful, our message to you is not "Yes and no." [19] For the Son of God, Jesus Christ, whom we proclaimed among you — Silvanus, Timothy, and I — did not become "Yes and no." On the contrary, in him it is always "Yes." [20] For every one of God's promises is "Yes" in him. Therefore, through him we also say "Amen" to the glory of God. [21] Now it is God who strengthens us together with you in Christ, and who has anointed us. [22] He has also put his seal on us and given us the Spirit in our hearts as a down payment.

[23] I call on God as a witness, on my life, that it was to spare you that I did not come to Corinth. [24] I do not mean that we lord it over your faith, but we are workers with you for your joy, because you stand firm in your faith. [1] In fact, I made up my mind about this: I would not come to you on another painful visit. [2] For if I cause you pain, then who will cheer me other than the one being hurt by me? [3] I wrote this very thing so that when I came I wouldn't have pain from those who ought to give me joy, because I am confident about all of you that my

joy will also be yours. **4** For I wrote to you with many tears out of an extremely troubled and anguished heart — not to cause you pain, but that you should know the abundant love I have for you.

A Sinner Forgiven

5 If anyone has caused pain, he has caused pain not so much to me but to some degree — not to exaggerate — to all of you. **6** This punishment by the majority is sufficient for that person. **7** As a result, you should instead forgive and comfort him. Otherwise, he may be overwhelmed by excessive grief. **8** Therefore I urge you to reaffirm your love to him. **9** I wrote for this purpose: to test your character to see if you are obedient in everything. **10** Anyone you forgive, I do too. For what I have forgiven — if I have forgiven anything — it is for your benefit in the presence of Christ, **11** so that we may not be taken advantage of by Satan. For we are not ignorant of his schemes.

A Trip to Macedonia

12 When I came to Troas to preach the gospel of Christ, even though the Lord opened a door for me, **13** I had no rest in my spirit because I did not find my brother Titus. Instead, I said good-bye to them and left for Macedonia.

A Ministry of Life or Death

14 But thanks be to God, who always leads us in Christ's triumphal procession and through us spreads the aroma of the knowledge of him in every place. **15** For to God we are the fragrance of Christ among those who are being saved and among those who are perishing. **16** To some we are an aroma of death leading to death, but to others, an aroma of life leading to life. Who is adequate for these things? **17** For we do not market the

word of God for profit like so many. On the contrary, we speak with sincerity in Christ, as from God and before God.

Living Letters

3 Are we beginning to commend ourselves again? Or do we need, like some, letters of recommendation to you or from you? ² You yourselves are our letter, written on our hearts, known and read by everyone. ³ You show that you are Christ's letter, delivered by us, not written with ink but with the Spirit of the living God — not on tablets of stone but on tablets of human hearts.

Paul's Competence

⁴ Such is the confidence we have through Christ before God. ⁵ It is not that we are competent in ourselves to claim anything as coming from ourselves, but our adequacy is from God. ⁶ He has made us competent to be ministers of a new covenant, not of the letter, but of the Spirit. For the letter kills, but the Spirit gives life.

New Covenant Ministry

⁷ Now if the ministry that brought death, chiseled in letters on stones, came with glory, so that the Israelites were not able to gaze steadily at Moses's face because of its glory, which was set aside, ⁸ how will the ministry of the Spirit not be more glorious? ⁹ For if the ministry that brought condemnation had glory, the ministry that brings righteousness overflows with even more glory. ¹⁰ In fact, what had been glorious is not glorious now by comparison because of the glory that surpasses it. ¹¹ For if what was set aside was glorious, what endures will be even more glorious.

¹² Since, then, we have such a hope, we act with great boldness. ¹³ We are not like Moses, who used to put a veil over his

face to prevent the Israelites from gazing steadily until the end of the glory of what was being set aside, ¹⁴ but their minds were hardened. For to this day, at the reading of the old covenant, the same veil remains; it is not lifted, because it is set aside only in Christ. ¹⁵ Yet still today, whenever Moses is read, a veil lies over their hearts, ¹⁶ but whenever a person turns to the Lord, the veil is removed. ¹⁷ Now the Lord is the Spirit, and where the Spirit of the Lord is, there is freedom. ¹⁸ We all, with unveiled faces, are looking as in a mirror at the glory of the Lord and are being transformed into the same image from glory to glory; this is from the Lord who is the Spirit.

The Light of the Gospel

4 Therefore, since we have this ministry because we were shown mercy, we do not give up. ² Instead, we have renounced secret and shameful things, not acting deceitfully or distorting the word of God, but commending ourselves before God to everyone's conscience by an open display of the truth. ³ But if our gospel is veiled, it is veiled to those who are perishing. ⁴ In their case, the god of this age has blinded the minds of the unbelievers to keep them from seeing the light of the gospel of the glory of Christ, who is the image of God. ⁵ For we are not proclaiming ourselves but Jesus Christ as Lord, and ourselves as your servants for Jesus's sake. ⁶ For God who said, "Let light shine out of darkness," has shone in our hearts to give the light of the knowledge of God's glory in the face of Jesus Christ.

Treasure in Clay Jars

⁷ Now we have this treasure in clay jars, so that this extraordinary power may be from God and not from us. ⁸ We are afflicted in every way but not crushed; we are perplexed but not in despair; ⁹ we are persecuted but not abandoned; we are struck down but not destroyed. ¹⁰ We always carry the death of Jesus

in our body, so that the life of Jesus may also be displayed in our body. **¹¹** For we who live are always being given over to death for Jesus's sake, so that Jesus's life may also be displayed in our mortal flesh. **¹²** So then, death is at work in us, but life in you. **¹³** And since we have the same spirit of faith in keeping with what is written, **I believed, therefore I spoke**, we also believe, and therefore speak. **¹⁴** For we know that the one who raised the Lord Jesus will also raise us with Jesus and present us with you. **¹⁵** Indeed, everything is for your benefit so that, as grace extends through more and more people, it may cause thanksgiving to increase to the glory of God.

¹⁶ Therefore we do not give up. Even though our outer person is being destroyed, our inner person is being renewed day by day. **¹⁷** For our momentary light affliction is producing for us an absolutely incomparable eternal weight of glory. **¹⁸** So we do not focus on what is seen, but on what is unseen. For what is seen is temporary, but what is unseen is eternal.

Our Future after Death

5 For we know that if our earthly tent we live in is destroyed, we have a building from God, an eternal dwelling in the heavens, not made with hands. **²** Indeed, we groan in this tent, desiring to put on our heavenly dwelling, **³** since, when we are clothed, we will not be found naked. **⁴** Indeed, we groan while we are in this tent, burdened as we are, because we do not want to be unclothed but clothed, so that mortality may be swallowed up by life. **⁵** Now the one who prepared us for this very purpose is God, who gave us the Spirit as a down payment.

⁶ So we are always confident and know that while we are at home in the body we are away from the Lord. **⁷** For we walk by faith, not by sight. **⁸** In fact, we are confident, and we would prefer to be away from the body and at home with the Lord. **⁹** Therefore, whether we are at home or away, we make it our

aim to be pleasing to him. ¹⁰ For we must all appear before the judgment seat of Christ, so that each may be repaid for what he has done in the body, whether good or evil.

¹¹ Therefore, since we know the fear of the Lord, we try to persuade people. What we are is plain to God, and I hope it is also plain to your consciences. ¹² We are not commending ourselves to you again, but giving you an opportunity to be proud of us, so that you may have a reply for those who take pride in outward appearance rather than in the heart. ¹³ For if we are out of our mind, it is for God; if we are in our right mind, it is for you. ¹⁴ For the love of Christ compels us, since we have reached this conclusion, that one died for all, and therefore all died. ¹⁵ And he died for all so that those who live should no longer live for themselves, but for the one who died for them and was raised.

The Ministry of Reconciliation

¹⁶ From now on, then, we do not know anyone from a worldly perspective. Even if we have known Christ from a worldly perspective, yet now we no longer know him in this way. ¹⁷ Therefore, if anyone is in Christ, he is a new creation; the old has passed away, and see, the new has come! ¹⁸ Everything is from God, who has reconciled us to himself through Christ and has given us the ministry of reconciliation. ¹⁹ That is, in Christ, God was reconciling the world to himself, not counting their trespasses against them, and he has committed the message of reconciliation to us.

²⁰ Therefore, we are ambassadors for Christ, since God is making his appeal through us. We plead on Christ's behalf, "Be reconciled to God." ²¹ He made the one who did not know sin to be sin for us, so that in him we might become the righteousness of God.

6 Working together with him, we also appeal to you, "Don't receive the grace of God in vain." ² For he says:

> At an acceptable time I listened to you,
> and in the day of salvation I helped you.

See, now is the acceptable time; now is the day of salvation!

The Character of Paul's Ministry

³ We are not giving anyone an occasion for offense, so that the ministry will not be blamed. ⁴ Instead, as God's ministers, we commend ourselves in everything: by great endurance, by afflictions, by hardships, by difficulties, ⁵ by beatings, by imprisonments, by riots, by labors, by sleepless nights, by times of hunger, ⁶ by purity, by knowledge, by patience, by kindness, by the Holy Spirit, by sincere love, ⁷ by the word of truth, by the power of God; through weapons of righteousness for the right hand and the left, ⁸ through glory and dishonor, through slander and good report; regarded as deceivers, yet true; ⁹ as unknown, yet recognized; as dying, yet see — we live; as being disciplined, yet not killed; ¹⁰ as grieving, yet always rejoicing; as poor, yet enriching many; as having nothing, yet possessing everything. ¹¹ We have spoken openly to you, Corinthians; our heart has been opened wide. ¹² We are not withholding our affection from you, but you are withholding yours from us. ¹³ I speak as to my children; as a proper response, open your heart to us.

Separation to God

¹⁴ Do not be yoked together with those who do not believe. For what partnership is there between righteousness and lawlessness? Or what fellowship does light have with darkness? ¹⁵ What agreement does Christ have with Belial? Or what does a believer have in common with an unbeliever? ¹⁶ And what agreement does the temple of God have with idols? For we are the temple of the living God, as God said:

> I will dwell
> and walk among them,

and I will be their God,
and they will be my people.
¹⁷ Therefore, come out from among them
and be separate, says the Lord;
do not touch any unclean thing,
and I will welcome you.
¹⁸ And I will be a Father to you,
and you will be sons and daughters to me,
says the Lord Almighty.

7 So then, dear friends, since we have these promises, let us cleanse ourselves from every impurity of the flesh and spirit, bringing holiness to completion in the fear of God.

Joy and Repentance

²Make room for us in your hearts. We have wronged no one, corrupted no one, taken advantage of no one. ³I don't say this to condemn you, since I have already said that you are in our hearts, to die together and to live together. ⁴I am very frank with you; I have great pride in you. I am filled with encouragement; I am overflowing with joy in all our afflictions.

⁵In fact, when we came into Macedonia, we had no rest. Instead, we were troubled in every way: conflicts on the outside, fears within. ⁶But God, who comforts the downcast, comforted us by the arrival of Titus, ⁷and not only by his arrival but also by the comfort he received from you. He told us about your deep longing, your sorrow, and your zeal for me, so that I rejoiced even more. ⁸For even if I grieved you with my letter, I don't regret it. And if I regretted it — since I saw that the letter grieved you, yet only for a while — ⁹I now rejoice, not because you were grieved, but because your grief led to repentance. For you were grieved as God willed, so that you didn't experience any loss from us. ¹⁰For godly

grief produces a repentance that leads to salvation without regret, but worldly grief produces death. ¹¹ For consider how much diligence this very thing — this grieving as God wills — has produced in you: what a desire to clear yourselves, what indignation, what fear, what deep longing, what zeal, what justice! In every way you showed yourselves to be pure in this matter. ¹² So even though I wrote to you, it was not because of the one who did wrong, or because of the one who was wronged, but in order that your devotion to us might be made plain to you in the sight of God. ¹³ For this reason we have been comforted.

In addition to our own comfort, we rejoiced even more over the joy Titus had, because his spirit was refreshed by all of you. ¹⁴ For if I have made any boast to him about you, I have not been disappointed; but as I have spoken everything to you in truth, so our boasting to Titus has also turned out to be the truth. ¹⁵ And his affection toward you is even greater as he remembers the obedience of all of you, and how you received him with fear and trembling. ¹⁶ I rejoice that I have complete confidence in you.

Appeal to Complete the Collection

8 We want you to know, brothers and sisters, about the grace of God that was given to the churches of Macedonia: ² During a severe trial brought about by affliction, their abundant joy and their extreme poverty overflowed in a wealth of generosity on their part. ³ I can testify that, according to their ability and even beyond their ability, of their own accord, ⁴ they begged us earnestly for the privilege of sharing in the ministry to the saints, ⁵ and not just as we had hoped. Instead, they gave themselves first to the Lord and then to us by God's will. ⁶ So we urged Titus that just as he had begun, so he should also complete among you this act of grace.

⁷ Now as you excel in everything — in faith, speech, knowledge, and in all diligence, and in your love for us — excel also in this act of grace. ⁸ I am not saying this as a command. Rather, by means of the diligence of others, I am testing the genuineness of your love. ⁹ For you know the grace of our Lord Jesus Christ: Though he was rich, for your sake he became poor, so that by his poverty you might become rich. ¹⁰ And in this matter I am giving advice because it is profitable for you, who began last year not only to do something but also to want to do it. ¹¹ Now also finish the task, so that just as there was an eager desire, there may also be a completion, according to what you have. ¹² For if the eagerness is there, the gift is acceptable according to what a person has, not according to what he does not have. ¹³ It is not that there should be relief for others and hardship for you, but it is a question of equality. ¹⁴ At the present time your surplus is available for their need, so that their abundance may in turn meet your need, in order that there may be equality. ¹⁵ As it is written: **The person who had much did not have too much, and the person who had little did not have too little.**

Administration of the Collection

¹⁶ Thanks be to God, who put the same concern for you into the heart of Titus. ¹⁷ For he welcomed our appeal and, being very diligent, went out to you by his own choice. ¹⁸ We have sent with him the brother who is praised among all the churches for his gospel ministry. ¹⁹ And not only that, but he was also appointed by the churches to accompany us with this gracious gift that we are administering for the glory of the Lord himself and to show our eagerness to help. ²⁰ We are taking this precaution so that no one will criticize us about this large sum that we are administering. ²¹ Indeed, we are giving careful thought to do what is right, not only before the Lord but also before people. ²² We have also sent with them our brother. We have often tested him

in many circumstances and found him to be diligent — and now even more diligent because of his great confidence in you. ²³ As for Titus, he is my partner and coworker for you; as for our brothers, they are the messengers of the churches, the glory of Christ. ²⁴ Therefore, show them proof before the churches of your love and of our boasting about you.

Motivations for Giving

9 Now concerning the ministry to the saints, it is unnecessary for me to write to you. ² For I know your eagerness, and I boast about you to the Macedonians, "Achaia has been ready since last year," and your zeal has stirred up most of them. ³ But I am sending the brothers so that our boasting about you in this matter would not prove empty, and so that you would be ready just as I said. ⁴ Otherwise, if any Macedonians come with me and find you unprepared, we, not to mention you, would be put to shame in that situation. ⁵ Therefore I considered it necessary to urge the brothers to go on ahead to you and arrange in advance the generous gift you promised, so that it will be ready as a gift and not as an extortion.

⁶ The point is this: The person who sows sparingly will also reap sparingly, and the person who sows generously will also reap generously. ⁷ Each person should do as he has decided in his heart — not reluctantly or out of compulsion, since God loves a cheerful giver. ⁸ And God is able to make every grace overflow to you, so that in every way, always having everything you need, you may excel in every good work. ⁹ As it is written:

He distributed freely;

he gave to the poor;

his righteousness endures forever.

¹⁰ Now the one who provides seed for the sower and bread for food will also provide and multiply your seed and increase the harvest of your righteousness. ¹¹ You will be enriched in every

way for all generosity, which produces thanksgiving to God through us. ¹² For the ministry of this service is not only supplying the needs of the saints but is also overflowing in many expressions of thanks to God. ¹³ Because of the proof provided by this ministry, they will glorify God for your obedient confession of the gospel of Christ, and for your generosity in sharing with them and with everyone. ¹⁴ And as they pray on your behalf, they will have deep affection for you because of the surpassing grace of God in you. ¹⁵ Thanks be to God for his indescribable gift!

Paul's Apostolic Authority

10 Now I, Paul, myself, appeal to you by the meekness and gentleness of Christ — I who am humble among you in person but bold toward you when absent. ² I beg you that when I am present I will not need to be bold with the confidence by which I plan to challenge certain people who think we are living according to the flesh. ³ For although we live in the flesh, we do not wage war according to the flesh, ⁴ since the weapons of our warfare are not of the flesh, but are powerful through God for the demolition of strongholds. We demolish arguments ⁵ and every proud thing that is raised up against the knowledge of God, and we take every thought captive to obey Christ. ⁶ And we are ready to punish any disobedience, once your obedience is complete.

⁷ Look at what is obvious. If anyone is confident that he belongs to Christ, let him remind himself of this: Just as he belongs to Christ, so do we. ⁸ For if I boast a little too much about our authority, which the Lord gave for building you up and not for tearing you down, I will not be put to shame. ⁹ I don't want to seem as though I am trying to terrify you with my letters. ¹⁰ For it is said, "His letters are weighty and powerful, but his physical presence is weak and his public speaking amounts

to nothing." **11** Let such a person consider this: What we are in our letters, when we are absent, we will also be in our actions when we are present.

12 For we don't dare classify or compare ourselves with some who commend themselves. But in measuring themselves by themselves and comparing themselves to themselves, they lack understanding. **13** We, however, will not boast beyond measure but according to the measure of the area of ministry that God has assigned to us, which reaches even to you. **14** For we are not overextending ourselves, as if we had not reached you, since we have come to you with the gospel of Christ. **15** We are not boasting beyond measure about other people's labors. On the contrary, we have the hope that as your faith increases, our area of ministry will be greatly enlarged, **16** so that we may preach the gospel to the regions beyond you without boasting about what has already been done in someone else's area of ministry. **17** So **let the one who boasts, boast in the Lord. 18** For it is not the one commending himself who is approved, but the one the Lord commends.

Paul and the False Apostles

11 I wish you would put up with a little foolishness from me. Yes, do put up with me! **2** For I am jealous for you with a godly jealousy, because I have promised you in marriage to one husband — to present a pure virgin to Christ. **3** But I fear that, as the serpent deceived Eve by his cunning, your minds may be seduced from a sincere and pure devotion to Christ. **4** For if a person comes and preaches another Jesus, whom we did not preach, or you receive a different spirit, which you had not received, or a different gospel, which you had not accepted, you put up with it splendidly!

5 Now I consider myself in no way inferior to those "super-apostles." **6** Even if I am untrained in public speaking, I am

certainly not untrained in knowledge. Indeed, we have in every way made that clear to you in everything. **7** Or did I commit a sin by humbling myself so that you might be exalted, because I preached the gospel of God to you free of charge? **8** I robbed other churches by taking pay from them to minister to you. **9** When I was present with you and in need, I did not burden anyone, since the brothers who came from Macedonia supplied my needs. I have kept myself, and will keep myself, from burdening you in any way. **10** As the truth of Christ is in me, this boasting of mine will not be stopped in the regions of Achaia. **11** Why? Because I don't love you? God knows I do!

12 But I will continue to do what I am doing, in order to deny an opportunity to those who want to be regarded as our equals in what they boast about. **13** For such people are false apostles, deceitful workers, disguising themselves as apostles of Christ. **14** And no wonder! For Satan disguises himself as an angel of light. **15** So it is no great surprise if his servants also disguise themselves as servants of righteousness. Their end will be according to their works.

Paul's Sufferings for Christ

16 I repeat: Let no one consider me a fool. But if you do, at least accept me as a fool so that I can also boast a little. **17** What I am saying in this matter of boasting, I don't speak as the Lord would, but as it were, foolishly. **18** Since many boast according to the flesh, I will also boast. **19** For you, being so wise, gladly put up with fools! **20** In fact, you put up with it if someone enslaves you, if someone exploits you, if someone takes advantage of you, if someone is arrogant toward you, if someone slaps you in the face. **21** I say this to our shame: We have been too weak for that!

But in whatever anyone dares to boast — I am talking foolishly — I also dare: **22** Are they Hebrews? So am I. Are they

Israelites? So am I. Are they the descendants of Abraham? So am I. ²³ Are they servants of Christ? I'm talking like a madman — I'm a better one: with far more labors, many more imprisonments, far worse beatings, many times near death.

²⁴ Five times I received the forty lashes minus one from the Jews. ²⁵ Three times I was beaten with rods. Once I received a stoning. Three times I was shipwrecked. I have spent a night and a day in the open sea. ²⁶ On frequent journeys, I faced dangers from rivers, dangers from robbers, dangers from my own people, dangers from Gentiles, dangers in the city, dangers in the wilderness, dangers at sea, and dangers among false brothers; ²⁷ toil and hardship, many sleepless nights, hunger and thirst, often without food, cold, and without clothing. ²⁸ Not to mention other things, there is the daily pressure on me: my concern for all the churches. ²⁹ Who is weak, and I am not weak? Who is made to stumble, and I do not burn with indignation?

³⁰ If boasting is necessary, I will boast about my weaknesses. ³¹ The God and Father of the Lord Jesus, who is blessed forever, knows I am not lying. ³² In Damascus, a ruler under King Aretas guarded the city of Damascus in order to arrest me. ³³ So I was let down in a basket through a window in the wall and escaped from his hands.

Sufficient Grace

12 Boasting is necessary. It is not profitable, but I will move on to visions and revelations of the Lord. ² I know a man in Christ who was caught up to the third heaven fourteen years ago. Whether he was in the body or out of the body, I don't know; God knows. ³ I know that this man — whether in the body or out of the body I don't know; God knows — ⁴ was caught up into paradise and heard inexpressible words, which a human being is not allowed to speak. ⁵ I will boast about this person, but not about myself, except of my weaknesses.

⁶ For if I want to boast, I wouldn't be a fool, because I would be telling the truth. But I will spare you, so that no one can credit me with something beyond what he sees in me or hears from me, ⁷ especially because of the extraordinary revelations. Therefore, so that I would not exalt myself, a thorn in the flesh was given to me, a messenger of Satan to torment me so that I would not exalt myself. ⁸ Concerning this, I pleaded with the Lord three times that it would leave me. ⁹ But he said to me, "My grace is sufficient for you, for my power is perfected in weakness."

Therefore, I will most gladly boast all the more about my weaknesses, so that Christ's power may reside in me. ¹⁰ So I take pleasure in weaknesses, insults, hardships, persecutions, and in difficulties, for the sake of Christ. For when I am weak, then I am strong.

Signs of an Apostle

¹¹ I have been a fool; you forced it on me. You ought to have commended me, since I am not in any way inferior to those "super-apostles," even though I am nothing. ¹² The signs of an apostle were performed with unfailing endurance among you, including signs and wonders and miracles. ¹³ So in what way are you worse off than the other churches, except that I personally did not burden you? Forgive me for this wrong!

Paul's Concern for the Corinthians

¹⁴ Look, I am ready to come to you this third time. I will not burden you, since I am not seeking what is yours, but you. For children ought not save up for their parents, but parents for their children. ¹⁵ I will most gladly spend and be spent for you. If I love you more, am I to be loved less? ¹⁶ Now granted, I did not burden you; yet sly as I am, I took you in by deceit! ¹⁷ Did I take advantage of you by any of those I sent you? ¹⁸ I urged Titus to

go, and I sent the brother with him. Titus didn't take advantage of you, did he? Didn't we walk in the same spirit and in the same footsteps?

[19] Have you been thinking all along that we were defending ourselves to you? No, in the sight of God we are speaking in Christ, and everything, dear friends, is for building you up. [20] For I fear that perhaps when I come I will not find you to be what I want, and you may not find me to be what you want. Perhaps there will be quarreling, jealousy, angry outbursts, selfish ambitions, slander, gossip, arrogance, and disorder. [21] I fear that when I come my God will again humiliate me in your presence, and I will grieve for many who sinned before and have not repented of the moral impurity, sexual immorality, and sensuality they practiced.

Final Warnings and Exhortations

13 This is the third time I am coming to you. **Every matter must be established by the testimony of two or three witnesses.** [2] I gave a warning when I was present the second time, and now I give a warning while I am absent to those who sinned before and to all the rest: If I come again, I will not be lenient, [3] since you seek proof of Christ speaking in me. He is not weak in dealing with you, but powerful among you. [4] For he was crucified in weakness, but he lives by the power of God. For we also are weak in him, but in dealing with you we will live with him by God's power.

[5] Test yourselves to see if you are in the faith. Examine yourselves. Or do you yourselves not recognize that Jesus Christ is in you? — unless you fail the test. [6] And I hope you will recognize that we ourselves do not fail the test. [7] But we pray to God that you do nothing wrong — not that we may appear to pass the test, but that you may do what is right, even though we may appear to fail. [8] For we can't do anything against the truth, but

only for the truth. [9] We rejoice when we are weak and you are strong. We also pray that you become fully mature. [10] This is why I am writing these things while absent, so that when I am there I may not have to deal harshly with you, in keeping with the authority the Lord gave me for building up and not for tearing down.

[11] Finally, brothers and sisters, rejoice. Become mature, be encouraged, be of the same mind, be at peace, and the God of love and peace will be with you. [12] Greet one another with a holy kiss. All the saints send you greetings.

[13] The grace of the Lord Jesus Christ, and the love of God, and the fellowship of the Holy Spirit be with you all.